AMANDA WHITTINGTON

Amanda Whittington was born in Nottingham in 1968. After leaving school, she worked as a freelance journalist for a variety of publications and was a columnist for the Nottingham Evening Post. Amanda's earliest plays – *Home Comforts* and *Stand Up Cherry Pye* – were staged by Takeaway Theatre in Nottingham pubs. She wrote *Twist and Shout* for Mansfield-based Young Perspectives, which was a hit at the 1998 National Youth Arts Festival and led to the commission of a sequel, *Runaway Girl*. The cigarette factory drama *Player's Angels* was written for New Perspectives and toured the East Midlands in 1999. *Be My Baby* was created as part of Soho Theatre Company's Writers' Development Programme. In 1998, it featured in Soho's 'Five Plays: Four Weeks' season at the Pleasance Theatre, London. *Be My Baby* was subsequently staged in the opening season of the Soho Theatre and Writers' Centre in May 2000.

Other titles in this series

AMANDA WHITTINGTON

Be My Baby

NICK HERN BOOKS

London

www.nickhernbooks.co.uk

A Nick Hern Book

Be My Baby first published in Great Britain in 2000
as a paperback original by Nick Hern Books Limited,
14 Larden Road, London W3 7ST

Be My Baby © 2000 by Amanda Whittington

Introduction copyright © 2000 by Amanda Whittington

Amanda Whittington has asserted her rights to be identified
as author of this work

Front cover design by Ned Hoste, 2H

Typeset by Country Setting, Kingsdown, Kent CT14 8ES

Printed and bound in Great Britain by Athenaeum Press Ltd,
Gateshead, Tyne and Wear

A CIP catalogue record for this book is available from
the British Library

ISBN 185459 489 3

Introduction

Be My Baby was commissioned by Soho Theatre in 1997 and
started life as the present-day story of a mother's reunion with
her adopted, grown-up child. Starting work on the play, I was
immediately faced with questions about the mother's past. Was
she unmarried? Who did she tell about the pregnancy? And
where did she go to have the baby?

Perhaps she had been packed off to one of the Church-run
maternity homes that were active in the 1960's? I set out to
look for some background information. Not surprisingly, I
found no Official History of Unmarried Mother and Baby
Homes. What I did discover were many 'first person' accounts
of such places in books and documentaries on adoption.

The sixties weren't swinging for these young women. They
spoke of being sent away like criminals, to live out their
pregnancy in secrecy and shame. The more I learned about
these homes, the more I knew it was a world I wanted to
explore. Hoping Soho Theatre wouldn't mind a few small
changes, I took the middle-aged mother of my story back
to where it all began. She became nineteen-year-old Mary
Adams – pregnant, unmarried and wanting only to keep her
baby. The play sets out to discover why she can't.

Setting *Be My Baby* in 1964 also gave the chance to include
some fantastic 'girl group' music by The Shangri-La's, The
Dixie Cups and the Ronettes. These three-minute pop dramas
seemed to perfectly capture the passionate innocence of the
play's characters – and gave an uplifting soundtrack to what
becomes a pretty dark tale.

I am extremely grateful to the birth mothers and adoptees who
spoke to me about their lives. *Be My Baby* is not the story of
one person or place. It draws on the many accounts I have
heard and read over three years of working on the play. During
this time, I was surprised by the number of people who told me

they or someone close to them had been touched by adoption. Many families, it seems, have their story to tell – and who knows how many more still keep the secret? I hope that in some way, *Be My Baby* speaks for them.

I would like to thank Abigail Morris and Paul Sirett of Soho Theatre for their guidance, encouragement and belief in the play. It would not have been written without them. *Be My Baby* is dedicated to my parents, who have always been there for me.

Amanda Whittington

Be My Baby was first presented by Soho Theatre Company at the Pleasance Theatre, London, on 10 November 1998, with the following cast:-

MARY	Kaye Wragg
QUEENIE	Lucy Speed
DOLORES	Naomi Radcliffe
NORMA	Anna Madeley
MATRON	Eleanor Bron
MRS ADAMS	Diana Quick

Director Abigail Morris
Designer Jonathan Fensom

The second production of *Be My Baby*, supported by the Peter Woolf Trust, was presented at the new Soho Theatre, Dean Street, London on 18 May 2000. At the time of going to press, the cast was as follows:-

MARY	Katie Blake
QUEENIE	Lucy Speed
DOLORES	Naomi Radcliffe
NORMA	Joanne Froggatt

Matron and Mrs. Adams were unconfirmed at time of press.

Director Abigail Morris
Designer Jonathan Fensom

The text of this production went to press before rehearsals, so may differ slightly from the play in performance.

Characters

MARY, *aged nineteen; seven months pregnant*

DOLORES, *aged seventeen; three months pregnant*

QUEENIE, *aged twenty; four months pregnant*

NORMA, *aged twenty; eight months pregnant*

MATRON, *Head of St Saviour's*

MRS ADAMS, *Mary's mother*

Be My Baby takes place over two months in 1964. It is set in
St Saviour's, a Church of England-run mother and baby home
in the North of England. St Saviour's takes in unmarried
mothers during their pregnancy and accommodates them until
their child is born and given up for adoption.

The austerity of St Saviour's is best suggested by a minimal set
comprising two single beds for the dormitory (with a door),
a small table and two chairs for Matron's study.

Featured singles are 'Be My Baby' by The Ronettes, 'Chapel
of Love' by The Dixie Cups, 'Past Present & Future' by The
Shangri-La's and 'So Young' by The Ronettes. More 'girl
groups' songs of the early 'sixties can be played between
scenes.

Scene One

*MARY's bedroom/MATRON's study. From a Dansette record
player comes the opening bars of Be My Baby by The Ronettes.
Beside the record player is an open suitcase belonging to
MARY ADAMS, who sits listening to the record, dressed in
her Sunday best. Enter MRS ADAMS, her equally well-
turned-out mother. MRS ADAMS packs a pile of clothes into
MARY's suitcase and closes it.*

*Enter MATRON, beginning another day at St Saviour's.
MATRON checks her hair in the mirror, sits at her desk, opens
a file and starts to read.*

*MRS ADAMS takes the needle off the record and closes the
lid. We hear the voices of QUEENIE, DOLORES and
NORMA, singing the final chorus to 'All Things Bright and
Beautiful'. MARY and MRS ADAMS button up their coats as
the girls start to pray.*

QUEENIE, DOLORES, NORMA. Almighty God; we give
thee humble thanks for that thou hast vouchsafed to deliver
Teresa thy servant from the great pain and peril of
childbirth.

*As an afterthought, MRS ADAMS puts MARY's teddy bear
into her handbag and picks up the suitcase. MARY takes a
last look at the Dansette.*

QUEENIE, DOLORES, NORMA. Grant, we beseech thee
most merciful Father that she, through thy help, may both
faithfully live and walk according to thy will, in this life
present; and also may be partaker of everlasting glory in the
life to come; through Jesus Christ our Lord . . .

MARY picks up the Dansette and follows MRS ADAMS.

QUEENIE, DOLORES, NORMA. Amen.

MARY and MRS ADAMS arrive at MATRON's study.

Scene Two

Study. MRS ADAMS *sits opposite* MATRON. MARY *stands by her side.*

MATRON. So her condition came to light . . .

MRS ADAMS. Yesterday, Matron.

MATRON. And she was last unwell . . .

MRS ADAMS. September.

MATRON. Seven months?

MRS ADAMS. She let out her clothes and took Mother for a fool.

MATRON. Has your doctor verified?

MRS ADAMS. There wasn't time.

MATRON. May I take his details . . .

MRS ADAMS. Why?

MATRON. To send for her notes.

MRS ADAMS. But he bowls with her father.

MATRON. Who hasn't been told?

MRS ADAMS. And won't be, with respect. He's put her on a pedestal, you see.

MATRON. You know why you're here, Mary?

MARY. Yes, Matron.

MATRON. Then you know what you've done?

MRS ADAMS. She knows far too much in my book.

MATRON *takes notes as* MARY *replies.*

MATRON. Full name?

MARY. Mary Elizabeth Adams.

MATRON. Date of birth?

MARY. I'm not sure, exactly. I haven't seen the doctor.

MATRON. *Your* birthday.

MRS ADAMS. Pay attention, Mary.

MARY. I'm sorry. March the first, 1945.

MATRON. Hair brown, eyes . . .

MRS ADAMS. Green.

MATRON. Height?

MARY. Erm . . .

MATRON. Five foot three or thereabouts. Church of England?

MRS ADAMS. Christened and confirmed.

MATRON. Education?

MRS ADAMS. Grammar school girl.

MATRON. Employment?

MRS ADAMS. Trustees Savings Bank. Junior Cashier.

MATRON. Illness or conditions?

MRS ADAMS. Just the usual childhood ailments.

MATRON. Our local GP has a temporary register. Should I make an appointment?

MRS ADAMS. Much appreciated.

MATRON. Are they holding her position in the bank?

MRS ADAMS. I'm to see the manager on Monday.

MATRON. Well, you can rest assured that she won't become idle. St Saviour's girls have to work for their keep.

MRS ADAMS. She's a willing kind of girl. Well, when I say willing . . .

MATRON. Our day begins with prayers at seven.

MRS ADAMS. I mean she was a Girl Guide.

MATRON. Breakfast is followed by general housework –
cooking, cleaning, laundry duties. Every girl takes her turn
on a rota.

MRS ADAMS. Forgive me Matron but I think you'll find her
different to the rest.

MATRON. All our girls are God's children, Mrs. Adams.

MRS ADAMS. Of course, Matron. But she gave in just the
once, she assures me of that.

MATRON. Afternoons are spent in welfare instruction.
Evenings are for recreation. Lights out at nine thirty.

MRS ADAMS. And the visiting hours?

MATRON. Not encouraged.

MRS ADAMS. I assumed the weekends?

MATRON. Buses are infrequent. And there's no Sunday
service.

MRS ADAMS. I expected to see her?

MATRON. It can be unsettling.

MRS ADAMS. To follow her progress.

MATRON. She's in good hands, Mrs. Adams.

MRS ADAMS. Of course. She's … she's brought her own
bedding.

MATRON. We take care of that.

MRS ADAMS. We didn't know the form.

MATRON. We take care of everything.

MRS ADAMS. Before and after?

MATRON. If that's what you require?

MRS ADAMS. She's nineteen, Matron.

MATRON. With a bright future.

MRS ADAMS. I don't want her paying all her life for one mistake.

MATRON. When the time comes, she'll be transferred to the General. Most girls return after nine or ten days, spend the night, collect their belongings and go home.

MARY. With the baby?

MATRON. The infant reverts to the care of Welfare Services, who place it for adoption.

MRS ADAMS. I don't know how it's come to this, I'm sure.

MATRON. Four guineas a week will take care of all her needs. If you wish to apply for social assistance . . .

MRS ADAMS. Thank you, no.

MATRON. We do ask for payment a week in advance.

MRS ADAMS *takes out four ten-pound notes and hands them to* MATRON.

MRS ADAMS. This should cover it.

MATRON. Weekly instalments are acceptable.

MRS ADAMS. It's my rule of thumb, Matron. Don't make the purchase if you can't pay the price.

MATRON. Registration.

MRS ADAMS. She'll be no trouble, I can promise you that.

MATRON *passes a form and a pen to* MRS ADAMS, *who signs it and hands it back.*

MATRON. Sign here, please.

MRS ADAMS. She's a good girl, really.

MATRON. With a good name to uphold.

MRS ADAMS. Pull your hair back so Matron can see you.

MARY *does as she's told.*

She's grateful you can take her, aren't you Mary?

MARY. Yes, Mother.

MRS ADAMS. You're a lucky girl, you know.

MARY. Yes, Mother.

MRS ADAMS. A very lucky girl.

MATRON *looks at her watch.*

MATRON. Quarter to twelve, Mary. Just time to make up your bed before lunch.

MRS ADAMS. Another job for Mother.

MATRON. Not at all, Mrs Adams. We can manage.

MRS ADAMS. With respect, Matron, you haven't seen her bedroom in the morning.

MATRON. I'm sure Mary can make a bed.

MRS ADAMS. Not to my standard.

MATRON. I've never seen a girl with so much luggage.

MARY. We weren't sure what I'd need.

MATRON. Only discipline and common sense. Follow me.

MATRON *exits, followed by* MRS ADAMS *and* MARY.

Scene Three

Laundry. Dressed in regulation pinafores, QUEENIE, NORMA *and* DOLORES *are scrubbing, rinsing and wringing out white bedsheets. 'Chapel of Love' by The Dixie Cups begins.* QUEENIE *sings along to the lead vocal, encouraging* DOLORES *and* NORMA *to join in. Standing side-by-side in the classic girl group pose, they dance and sing along to the song, which is played in its entirety.*

Scene Four

Dormitory. MRS ADAMS *is making one of the two beds with military precision.*

MARY. Can I give you a hand?

MRS ADAMS. You can't do corners.

MARY. Suppose I ought to learn.

MRS ADAMS. You can say that again.

MARY *unpacks her suitcase. She looks at the other bed.*

MARY. I hope she's nice, the other girl. I hope she's easy.

MRS ADAMS. You can count on it.

MARY. We might even be friends?

MRS ADAMS. You keep your counsel. The last thing your father needs is some little tramp turning up on the doorstep.

MARY. What will you tell him?

MRS ADAMS. We had a call from the country. Your Aunt's had a fall. Asked for Mary.

MARY. And you'll say the same at the bank?

MRS ADAMS. You'll be quite the little heroine.

MARY. What about Jonathan?

MRS ADAMS *turns down the corners of the bed.*

MRS ADAMS. Fold once and twice and under.

MARY. Will you tell him where I am?

MRS ADAMS. And then lift the end up for your toes.

MARY. Mother?

MRS ADAMS. I won't hear anyone say you weren't shown the way.

MARY. He loves me.

MRS ADAMS. Is this what you do to someone you love?

MARY. We had no idea it would end up like this.

MRS ADAMS. He's a medical student. Heaven help his patients.

MARY. If you'd just give him a chance . . .

MRS ADAMS. A chance? When all he's given you is a past?

Enter MATRON, *with a small pile of clothes.*

MATRON. One pinafore, one blouse.

MARY. Thank you, Matron.

MATRON. The girls are having lunch, Mary. They've put aside a plate.

MRS ADAMS. Take the end, Mary.

MARY *helps* MRS ADAMS *straighten the blankets across the bed.*

MATRON. Bible class begins at two. And there's a bus at the end of the lane in ten minutes.

MRS ADAMS *looks at her watch then at* MARY.

MRS ADAMS. Is that the time? It goes so fast.

MATRON. The 37 heads directly to the station.

MRS ADAMS. Did I . . . did I mention onions?

MATRON. I'm sorry?

MRS ADAMS. She can't eat onions. Bring her out in a rash. From being a child.

MARY. It's all right, Mother. I'll pick them out.

MRS ADAMS. You packed the soap?

MARY. Will you be all right on the train?

MRS ADAMS. And a nice new flannel like I said?

MARY. I can lend you a book . . .

MRS ADAMS. Keep yourself clean. It's important.

MARY. I'll write . . .

MRS ADAMS *shakes her head.*

MRS ADAMS. Your father.

MARY. Telephone?

MATRON *helps* MRS ADAMS *into her coat.*

MRS ADAMS. Just do as you're told and you'll come to no harm.

MARY. Will you be all right?

MRS ADAMS. Time's pressing . . .

MARY. On the bus, I mean. Without me.

MRS ADAMS. It's for the best, Mary.

MARY. Are you sure you'll be all right?

MRS ADAMS. For the best.

MRS ADAMS *pulls* MARY*'s teddy bear from her handbag, sits it on* MARY*'s bed and exits, followed by* MATRON. MARY *takes a crumpled bag of boiled sweets from her coat pocket.*

MARY. Mother?

Enter MATRON. MARY *gives her the bag.*

MATRON. You'll disturb the other girls.

MARY. She's forgotten the sweets.

MATRON. Just put on your pinafore and come to . . .

MARY. But she's travel sick, they help.

MATRON. You want to help your mother?

MARY. She suffers with her nerves.

MATRON. Then don't cause a scene.

Exit MATRON, *with the sweets.* MARY *puts on her pinafore. She takes a pile of 45 records from her suitcase and opens the lid of the Dansette. Enter* QUEENIE. *She studies* MARY, *who is unaware of her presence.* QUEENIE *lights a cigarette.*

QUEENIE. Do you take requests?

MARY *turns in surprise.*

MARY. What do you like?

QUEENIE. Nowt you've got.

MARY. I might.

QUEENIE. Bobby Sox and the Blue Jeans?

MARY. 'Not Too Young To Get Married.'

QUEENIE. Dixie Cups?

MARY. 'Chapel of Love.'

QUEENIE. The Ronettes?

MARY. What's your favourite?

QUEENIE. 'Be My Baby.'

MARY *finds 'Be My Baby' among the singles and hands it to* QUEENIE.

MARY. Are we sharing?

QUEENIE. You better believe it.

MARY. I'm Mary.

QUEENIE. Where's your little lamb?

MARY. I lost it.

QUEENIE *picks up the teddy bear on* MARY'*s bed.*

QUEENIE. And who's this?

MARY. Mrs Farren.

QUEENIE. Mrs Who?

MARY. Farren. After the neighbour who gave her to me. I've always slept with it.

QUEENIE. By the look of you, that's not the only one.

MARY. I've got a steady boyfriend.

QUEENIE. Buy you all them love songs, did he?

MARY. He likes to surprise me.

QUEENIE. You can say that again.

QUEENIE *looks again at the record.*

MARY. I've got all their 45s, The Ronettes. I hope they don't put one out while I'm in here.

QUEENIE. Could have been me, this. Top of the hit parade.

MARY. Can you sing?

QUEENIE. Met a bloke who said I'd got what it takes. Then what I'd got, he took.

QUEENIE *offers her cigarette to* MARY.

I'm Queenie.

MARY. Are you allowed?

QUEENIE. No.

MARY. But what about Matron?

QUEENIE. You're not scared of the holy cow, are you?

MARY. She might come up.

QUEENIE. So what if she does?

MARY. I don't want to get into trouble.

QUEENIE. Bit late for that, duck. Let's hear it.

QUEENIE *offers the record to* MARY.

MARY. Shouldn't we ask permission?

QUEENIE *goes to the Dansette, puts on 'Be My Baby' and grins at* MARY, *who can't help but smile back.*

Scene Five

Laundry. Two weeks later. QUEENIE *and* MARY *are washing sheets whilst* DOLORES *and* NORMA *each read from a teen annual and a medical book.*

DOLORES. 'Which are the great days in a girl's life? A hard question to answer but you can be sure that on her greatest days, there will be a boy in the picture somewhere . . . '

NORMA. 'The actual onset of labour is probably governed by the endocrine secretion of the posterior part of the pituitary gland.'

DOLORES. 'First Date is one of the millstones in a girl's life.'

MARY. Milestones.

DOLORES. 'The day she stops being a child and becomes a woman. This is why the first date should be a happy affair – but it won't if you go all . . . all . . . '

DOLORES *shows the magazine to* MARY.

MARY. Neurotic, Doll.

DOLORES. Did you go neurotic?

MARY. No, I went dancing.

DOLORES. Me and Alfie went dancing. Round and round our yard to the wireless.

MARY. Jonathan took me to the Palais on our first date.

DOLORES. Is that where you met him?

QUEENIE. Am I the only scrubber left in this laundry?

MARY. I used to sit behind him on the bus home from work. Couldn't take my eyes off the back of his neck. Eventually he turned, walked me home and we never looked back.

DOLORES *returns to her book.*

DOLORES. 'Saying goodnight to your date is left to your good taste and judgement – and to the way you have been brought up.'

NORMA. 'This finally overcomes the opposite
the progesterone and placental hormones.'

DOLORES. 'Remember as you say goodbye a
that your date wants to respect you as well

NORMA. 'And produces the rhythmic, painful contrac...
labour.'

DOLORES. 'Deep inside, he wants you to reject his offer of a
goodnight kiss.'

MARY. Painful?

DOLORES. 'Even if his actions may not support that idea.'

MARY. Painful like a headache? Toothache? Earache?

QUEENIE. I'll give you earache if you don't get working.

DOLORES. 'Ey, Norma? Is there owt on wind?

QUEENIE. I've heard we're due for rain.

DOLORES. In your doctor's book. Between you and me, I've
had shocking wind.

MARY. I can't stop spending a penny.

NORMA. It bears down on the bladder.

MARY. Bears down?

NORMA. The uterus.

MARY. Uterus?

NORMA. Womb.

DOLORES. You what?

NORMA. What the baby's in, look.

    NORMA *shows* DOLORES *a picture in the book.*

DOLORES. It's upside down.

    NORMA *puts her hands to her stomach, looking at the
    picture.*

NORMA. I think the head's somewhere here.

DOLORES. *(reading)* 'As the muscle of the u-ter-us contracts, the neck of the bag, or cervix, is drawn up and widened. Soon this bag bursts . . . '

MARY. Bursts?

DOLORES. 'Its contained water flows away and the fo-etus . . . '

DOLORES *looks up.* NORMA, MARY *and* QUEENIE *reply in unison.*

DOLORES, QUEENIE, NORMA. Baby.

DOLORES. 'The fo-etus is expelled'.

MARY. What does it mean 'bursts'?

DOLORES. My Alfie were expelled from school.

QUEENIE. Like a great big ugly boil.

MARY. Does it make a mess?

QUEENIE. There's all sorts comes out.

MARY. Like what?

QUEENIE. Like pus and blood . . .

MARY. Blood?

NORMA. There's nothing here on blood.

DOLORES. I faint at the sight.

MARY. All right, there's bound to be a bit …

NORMA. There's no mention in the book.

DOLORES. But there won't be much? Queen, I can't do it if there's much?

QUEENIE. Get back to work.

The girls continue working.

NORMA. My friend cut his finger once. Broken glass in the storeroom. He was a big man but there were tears in his eyes. I kissed his hand to make it go away.

QUEENIE. What friend's this then, Norma?

MARY. Boyfriend, is it?

QUEENIE. Come on, Norma. Mary's only been here a
fortnight and we know about Johnny from his shoe size up.

MARY. Jonathan.

DOLORES. She don't talk about it.

QUEENIE. Well, it's about time she did. What kind of friend?

NORMA. Not your kind.

QUEENIE. Perfect gentleman, was he?

NORMA. Yes.

QUEENIE. 'Course he was. That's why you're in here.

The girls continue working.

DOLORES. Suppose it's bound to when you think of it.

MARY. What?

DOLORES. Start bleeding. When they cut your tummy for the
baby.

MARY. They don't cut you, do they?

QUEENIE. Not where she thinks.

DOLORES. Well, how else does it come out?

*MARY goes to DOLORES and guides her hands onto her
stomach. NORMA puts down her book and listens to
MARY.*

MARY. This is the baby. Upside down . . .

DOLORES. Like in the picture?

MARY. They don't cut you. I think it sort-of drops out.

DOLORES. Where from?

QUEENIE. Same way it went in.

DOLORES looks down at herself then up at MARY.

DOLORES. A baby comes out there?

QUEENIE. You've heard of that camel through the eye of a needle?

DOLORES. A whole baby?

MARY. It stretches, I think. Like putting on a sweater.

DOLORES. So they don't cut you open?

MARY. No.

DOLORES. In't that a relief?

QUEENIE. For the last time: am I the only scrubber left in this laundry?

The girls continue working.

DOLORES. Queen . . .

QUEENIE. What?

DOLORES. Giz a ciggie?

QUEENIE. Gerrup your own end.

DOLORES. You promised . . .

QUEENIE. You're not allowed.

DOLORES. Why?

QUEENIE. It kills your brain cells.

DOLORES. Does it?

QUEENIE. And seeing as you've only got the one . . .

QUEENIE *throws a sheet over* DOLORES.

DOLORES. I'll have an accident.

QUEENIE. Y'are a bloody accident.

DOLORES *pulls off the sheet.*

DOLORES. Smashing, in't it?

MARY. What's that, Doll?

DOLORES. Us lot. In here. Up the duff.

Scene Six

Study. A month later. MATRON *opens a compact mirror and neatly retouches her lipstick. There is a knock on the door.*

MATRON. Come.

> MATRON *snaps the compact shut. Enter* MARY, *clutching a copy of* The Lady *magazine and a letter.*

MARY. Matron?

MATRON. Mary?

MARY. I'd like a day off.

MATRON. A particular day – or will any one do?

MARY. Next Wednesday, Matron. I've got an interview.

> MARY *gives the magazine, folded open, for* MATRON *to read.*

MATRON. 'Housekeeper required for elderly lady, Eastbourne. Light domestic duties and companionship. Own room. Child considered.'

MARY. And I'm experienced now. Domestically.

MATRON. You've contacted the lady?

MARY. She wrote back by return of post.

MATRON. And does she know your situation?

MARY. I thought it best to tell her face to face.

MATRON. Sit down, Mary.

MARY. So she could see what kind of girl I am.

MATRON. You're a clever girl, Mary. Five 'O' levels, I'm told.

MARY. Imagine living by the sea.

MATRON. And raised for more than service.

> MATRON *passes the magazine back to* MARY.

MARY. But it takes care of everything.

MATRON. Except the child.

MARY. Especially the child.

MATRON. Let's assume he feeds at four-hourly intervals; round the clock, two, six and ten. Each feed will take you, say, thirty minutes each. In between, you'll bathe him, dress him, comfort him. How will you housekeep with a baby on your hip?

MARY. My cousin's got a baby. Her house is immaculate.

MATRON. And what else has your cousin got?

MARY. A twin-tub?

MATRON. A husband.

   MARY *opens the letter and offers it to* MATRON.

MARY. She lives on her own. She might take to a baby in the house?

   MATRON *reads the letter and hands it back.*

MATRON. Why don't you ask her?

MARY. Now?

MATRON. She won't thank you for wasting her time.

   MARY *dials the telephone on* MATRON*'s desk.*

MARY. It's ringing.

   Hello, Mrs Wilson . . . This is Mary Adams, you wrote to me regarding an interview . . . well, I'm just ringing to say that I'd very much like to attend . . . two o'clock's fine, yes . . . I look forward to meeting you too, except . . . the thing is Mrs Wilson, I'm . . . I'm in hospital at the moment . . . nothing serious, no . . . I'm having a baby . . . a baby, yes . . . no, I'm not a widow . . . that's correct, Mrs Wilson. Unmarried . . . well, because of 'child considered' . . . but I am suitable . . . are you sure you wouldn't like me to . . . I see . . . I'm sorry . . . thank you, Mrs Wilson . . . goodbye.

MARY *replaces the receiver and looks again at the magazine.*

MARY. There's plenty more here.

MATRON. Try one.

MARY *dials another number. She waits for a reply but finally puts the phone down.*

MARY. No reply.

MATRON. Try another.

MARY *dials again.*

MARY. 'Hello . . . Hello, yes, my name's Mary Adams and I'm ringing about your advertisement in *The Lady* . . . has the position been filled . . . oh, good . . . you say you'd take someone with a child . . . only a girl . . . well, I'm not sure what it is yet, I haven't had it, you see . . . aged five and over . . . oh . . . thank you very much . . . goodbye.

MARY *puts the phone down.*

MATRON. You've got a job, Mary. And a home to go back to.

MARY. I know, Matron. But the thing is, I can feel it moving. I can feel it moving and I'm scared, you see . . .

MATRON. Quite natural.

MARY. I'm scared I'm going to love it.

Pause.

MATRON. And what kind of love is that, Mary?

MARY. What kind?

MATRON. The kind of love that takes – or the kind of love that gives?

MARY. Just love.

MATRON. What else can you offer your child, Mary? A Christian home? Financial security? A legitimate name?

MARY. I thought Matthew for a boy. Lucy for a girl.

MATRON. And Matthew or Lucy – what do they need?

MARY *struggles for an answer.*

What does a child need, Mary?

MARY. Milk?

MATRON. Milk.

MARY. Toys?

MATRON. Toys.

MARY. Nappies.

MATRON. And who provides the milk and toys and napkins?

MATRON *gives* MARY *time to think of a reply.*

A father.

MARY. He said he'd marry me. Once he's qualified. He's going to be a doctor. I won't stand in his way. I'll stand on my own two feet from now on.

MATRON. How?

MARY. I've got a job, I'll find a room.

MATRON. Alone?

MARY. With the baby.

MATRON. I've seen those rooms, Mary. Damp rooms on the wrong side of town. Three flights up, old gas fire, washing never quite gets dry. Underweight babies raised on small change and handouts and the pity of friends. Girls who try to live from day to day – and end up passed from man to man.

MARY. I'd never get to that.

MATRON. Leave here with your baby and you're halfway there.

MARY *looks at the telephone.*

MARY. Not if I went home.

MATRON. To your father's house?

MARY. It's his grandchild.

MATRON. And would he want to see it raised without a name?

MARY. Better than not seeing it at all.

MATRON. Better for whom, Mary?

MARY looks at the time.

MARY. It's ten past three.

MATRON. For the child?

MARY. I can speak to him at work.

MARY reaches for the telephone and dials.

MATRON. For you?

MARY. If he says yes, can I go home today?

MATRON. But if he says no, can you ever?

MARY. He's got a right to know.

MATRON. And what would that do to your mother?

MARY puts the telephone down.

MATRON. I met a lady and gentlemen last week. Beautiful house on the coast. Desperate for a child of their own. After ten years, they say the hardest thing is losing hope.

There is a knock on the door.

MATRON. Come . . .

Enter NORMA.

NORMA. Excuse me, Matron.

MATRON. Later, Norma.

NORMA. But I've wet myself. It won't stop.

MATRON. When?

NORMA. About half an hour ago.

MATRON. Mary – fetch Norma's overnight bag.

MARY. Is she all right, Matron?

MATRON. She will be. Run along.

Exit MARY.

MATRON. Lie down, Norma.

NORMA. I couldn't hold it back.

MATRON. Let's take a look at you.

MATRON *examines* NORMA.

NORMA. It's all over the floor.

MATRON. We'll mop it up.

NORMA. Does it mean there's something wrong?

MATRON. You'll live.

NORMA. Is it 'cos of the pills?

MATRON. You won't help yourself by making a fuss.

NORMA. Have I hurt it with the pills?

MATRON. What pills?

NORMA. Big black ones. Twelve to a box. He never said what was in them. I've studied that book but I can't find what they were.

MATRON. When?

NORMA. The firm made deliveries to a pharmacist. He had a word with the chemist, left the box inside my desk. Where he'd put those little notes at the beginning. Then his letters. A white rose. And the money . . . the money . . . the money to come here . . .

MATRON. You won't have harmed the baby.

NORMA. I took the pills, though. And when they didn't work, I . . .

MATRON. What?

NORMA. Oh, Matron. I swore not to tell but I should,
    shouldn't I?

MATRON. If you've harmed yourself, yes.

NORMA. He took me to a woman, she lived above a shop. She
    laid me down, brought a syringe . . .

    NORMA *cries out in pain.*

MATRON. What was in the syringe, Norma?

NORMA. I can't remember. It began with a C.

MATRON. Carbolic.

NORMA. We were scared to do it but more scared not to. He
    held my hand like he was holding me down.

MATRON. What kind of a man was he?

NORMA. Married.

Scene Seven

Laundry. A week later. QUEENIE, MARY *and* DOLORES *are
at work.*

DOLORES. And so I says to Alfie 'you want to see me bottom
    drawer'? He says 'can I' so I says 'come up'. He says 'your
    Mam's out' and I say 'yeah but it don't mean your luck's
    in'. So he follows me up and I shows him what I'd got.

QUEENIE. What's that then, Doll?

DOLORES. Set of knives and forks off the market, yellow
    vase from when me Auntie died and a lovely blue bedspread
    what me Mam made. 'We'll be cosy under there', says Alf,
    'cheeky bogger' says I. When me Mam got back, I told her
    what he says and she says 'there you go. He wants to name
    the day.'

MARY. And did he?

QUEENIE. Tenth of Julember, in't it, Doll?

DOLORES. I says 'I don't want a big 'un, Mam, it won't cost
you nowt', 'that's just as well', she says . I says 'how's
about what our Brenda got wed in, it's been worn just the
once' but it turns out she dyed it red for her twenty-first.
'Well,' me Mam says. 'Looks like I'll be getting out me
needle and thread'.

QUEENIE. Combine it with a christening, Doll. Two for the
price of one.

DOLORES. Do I have to have it christened?

QUEENIE. Goes to the devil if you don't.

DOLORES. Won't the lady who has it have it christened?

MARY. I suppose she will.

DOLORES. Matron says she's giving it a name.

MARY. I'm naming mine.

DOLORES. I'd have Cliff for a boy and Cilla for a girl.

QUEENIE. You can't call a kid Cilla.

DOLORES. She did.

QUEENIE. Who?

DOLORES. Mrs Black.

MARY. That's short for Priscilla.

DOLORES. Like Queenie?

QUEENIE. No, duck. That's long for Queen.

The girls continue working.

DOLORES. What do you think Norma's called hers?

Silence.

Do you reckon her fella were there?

MARY. Where?

DOLORES. At the hospital.

QUEENIE. She won't see him for dust.

DOLORES. He was here every Friday.

QUEENIE. In her head.

DOLORES. Parked down the lane after lights out.

QUEENIE. You've kept this to yourself.

DOLORES. She told me not to say owt but it don't matter does it, now she's gone?

MARY. Did he come in?

DOLORES. He'd just sit there looking. And she'd look back. Never said owt. Then one night, he weren't there. First she says he's had an accident, next she thinks he's told his wife.

MARY. He's married?

DOLORES. But she never stopped waiting at that window.

QUEENIE. Little madam.

DOLORES. They're coming to me wedding 'cos no-one'll know him.

QUEENIE. Always the quiet ones, in't it?

DOLORES. She's going to be me bridesmaid.

QUEENIE. Norma?

DOLORES. What's wrong with that?

QUEENIE. She's a bad girl, Doll. Fallen woman. Slut.

MARY. In your language.

QUEENIE. Means summat good where I come from. Means you can have a laugh, pick up a lad and drop him when it suits. Means you take care of yourself.

MARY. Really? So how come you've ended up in here?

QUEENIE *turns away.* DOLORES *starts to sing the chorus of 'Chapel of Love'.*

QUEENIE. You know what, Dolores? I'd like to know why this knight-in-shining-bloody-armour's not made an honest woman of you?

DOLORES. I am honest.

QUEENIE. You could have wed once you'd fell; set yourself up in your mam's back room. I mean, you've got the bloody bedspread.

DOLORES. He wants to have us own house.

QUEENIE. But not your own kid?

DOLORES *continues singing 'Chapel of Love'*.

QUEENIE. You're no more going to the chapel than going to the moon.

MARY. Leave her . . .

QUEENIE. You've not even got a lad, have yer?

DOLORES. 'Course I have.

QUEENIE. Then where is he?

DOLORES. At home.

QUEENIE. He had his way – then he were on his way.

DOLORES. He did never.

QUEENIE. Then who gave you that, Father Christmas?

DOLORES. The lad from packing.

DOLORES *continues her washing.*

MARY. Doll?

DOLORES. Yeah?

MARY. What lad from packing?

DOLORES. Alfie were meeting us from work but he were late and it were dark. Then out comes this lad from packing. I were chilly so he took us for a drink. Cherry brandy, it were smashing. Walked me home across the wreck. He started . . . I said stop . . . I liked him . . . well, it were over quick enough.

MARY. Does Alfie know?

DOLORES. When I got in, he'd been out looking. Said he'd fetch a policeman but Mam said I'd be in bother. She said to go home and say no more about it. So he did.

MARY. And have you seen him since?

DOLORES. I've been in here, an't I?

DOLORES *continues washing.*

MARY. We should tell Matron . . .

QUEENIE. Forget it.

MARY. But it's . . .

QUEENIE. Over and done with.

MARY. So the lad from packing gets away with it?

QUEENIE. She took the drink, she let him walk her home. I dare say she were curious.

MARY. Curious? I'd say she was . . .

QUEENIE. What?

MARY. Treated like dirt.

QUEENIE. And you were Snow-bleeding-White?

MARY. We'd been together two years. We were going to get married.

QUEENIE. Listen, love: we all come here with that dirt on our hands. Not even them little white gloves of yours can hide it.

MARY. At least I'm not wearing it like warpaint.

DOLORES. He can't come like Norma's lad. He's not got a car. He'll just be waiting, won't he?

Pause.

MARY. 'Course he will.

QUEENIE *starts to sing 'Chapel of Love'.* MARY *and* DOLORES *join in.*

Scene Eight

Study. Enter NORMA. MATRON *gestures for her to sit down.*

MATRON. Good news, Norma. Welfare Services have located a family in Coventry.

NORMA. Coventry? Is that near here?

MATRON. Professional people. The husband's an accountant.

NORMA. Will he be their first?

MATRON. They have a little girl, aged three.

NORMA. Someone to play with.

MATRON. A lifetime companion.

NORMA. What if he doesn't fit in?

MATRON. He's just the same colouring. Blue eyes like the girl.

NORMA. Blue eyes?

MATRON. He'll be part of a family, Norma. Raised as their own.

NORMA. An accountant, you say? With figures?

MATRON. And a thriving practice.

NORMA. What if he takes after me? I'm hopeless at maths.

MATRON. They're very grateful to you, Norma. A healthy baby boy.

NORMA. He's healthy?

MATRON. Perfectly.

NORMA. Are you sure?

MATRON. Norma, you've had plenty of time to put this out of your mind.

NORMA. I've tried, Matron.

MATRON. It's time to look forward.

NORMA. I will. I am.

MATRON. I hope we've helped you, Norma?

NORMA. I'm grateful for everything you've done.

MATRON. Is anyone meeting you tomorrow?

NORMA. Tomorrow, Matron?

MATRON. Will anyone go with you?

NORMA. What exactly am I doing tomorrow?

MATRON. Signing the papers.

NORMA. Then I'll get to see him?

MATRON. You'll get to go home.

NORMA. I can't go home, Matron. He won't know where I am.

MATRON. Who won't?

NORMA. Coventry.

MATRON. Has the procedure not been explained to you, Norma?

NORMA. Procedure?

MATRON. Welfare Services will place your baby with his new family in Coventry. In due course, the Magistrates Court . . .

NORMA. Have I done wrong?

MATRON. The Magistrates Court will pass what is called a Consent to Adoption Order. This makes your baby the legitimate child of the adoptive parents. Their name will replace yours on the certificate of birth . . .

NORMA. What is their name?

MATRON. This means you have no legal right to contact your child.

NORMA. Until he's settled in?

MATRON. I'm sorry, Norma. You have no right to contact your child.

NORMA. But what if we get married?

MATRON. I hope you will get married. But not to someone else's husband.

NORMA *starts to cry.*

MATRON. Did the tablets dry your milk up, Norma?

NORMA. Yes, Matron.

MATRON *hands her a tissue.*

MATRON. Don't let the other girls see you like this.

NORMA. I won't.

MATRON. We don't want to worry them.

NORMA. I have done wrong.

MATRON. Perhaps we'll bring you back here tomorrow? A few days in the sick room might give you a rest.

NORMA. I'm going to hell, aren't I?

MATRON. Who on earth's told you that?

NORMA. I am. I know I am.

MATRON. Norma, listen ....

NORMA. Oh God, I'm going to hell.

MATRON *takes* NORMA*'s hand and begins to say the Lord's Prayer, encouraging* NORMA *to say it with her.*

MATRON, NORMA. Our Father, who art in heaven, hallowed be thy name. Thy kingdom come, thy will be done, on earth as it is in heaven. Give us this day our daily bread and forgive us our trespasses, as we forgive those who trespass against us. Lead us not into temptation but deliver us from evil. For thine is the kingdom, the power and the glory, for ever and ever, Amen.

Scene Nine

Dormitory. QUEENIE *and* MARY *are in bed, seemingly asleep, until* QUEENIE *starts singing 'Be My Baby'.* MARY *joins in the chorus.*

QUEENIE. You never said you had pipes?

MARY. I haven't.

QUEENIE. They sound all right to me.

MARY. I couldn't even make the school choir.

QUEENIE. I couldn't make school in the end. I'd stop at home and help me Mam.

MARY. I wish I'd been more like you. I wish I hadn't taken it so seriously.

QUEENIE. You came out with exams, though. They get you places, do exams.

MARY. You're going places.

QUEENIE. Am I?

MARY. Top of the hit parade, remember.

QUEENIE. I thought I had me ticket out, once upon a time. I waited at the stop but the bus never came.

MARY. What are you on about?

QUEENIE. We're friends, aren't we?

MARY. You know we are.

QUEENIE. You'd tell me the truth if I asked?

MARY. And nothing but.

QUEENIE. Well, I'm asking. Can I sing?

MARY. You just have.

QUEENIE. I know – but can I sing good?

MARY. Depends what you mean by good?

QUEENIE. Like Ronnie Spector?

MARY. No-one sings like Ronnie, Queen.

QUEENIE *gets out of bed to look through* MARY*'s singles.*

QUEENIE. What would you ask her if she walked in here now?

MARY. I don't think that's likely.

QUEENIE. Imagine she did. What would you say if she did?

MARY. What would you?

QUEENIE. 'Take me with you. I don't care where you're going, just take me'.

MARY. 'I fell in love to your music'. I'd like to tell her that.

QUEENIE. With Johnny?

MARY. We had his flat to ourselves every Friday.

QUEENIE. Was he your first?

MARY. Of course. Wasn't yours?

QUEENIE. Yeah, course.

MARY. I told Mother we went dancing. I know it was bad – but Queenie, it was good.

QUEENIE. Too good to last, eh?

MARY. He came for me the night I was packing. Mother stopped him at the gate. I don't know what she said but he left without a word.

QUEENIE. Mine said he'd stand by me – 'til me Dad knocked him off his feet.

MARY. Not even a look to the bedroom window.

QUEENIE *finds a record and puts it on the turntable.*

QUEENIE. Went down on one knee, the works. He'd been at sea since he were fifteen. I daresay he wanted summat to come home to. He were sorting out one of them navy homes and everything.

MARY. Why didn't you say yes?

QUEENIE. He'd only know us six weeks. It'd have worn off then we'd be just like all the rest.

QUEENIE *plays 'Past Present & Future' by The Shangri-La's. They listen to the 'past' verse and join in with the 'present', speaking the lines to each other melodramatically as the story unfolds.* QUEENIE *holds out her hand to* MARY *and they waltz around the bedroom to the instrumental part. Enter* DOLORES *and* NORMA, *bringing an abrupt end to the dance.*

DOLORES. Queen?

QUEENIE *turns the record off.*

QUEENIE. Bleedin' hell, Doll. I thought you were the holy cow.

DOLORES. Them stairs are pitch black.

QUEENIE *looks at* NORMA.

QUEENIE. What's she doing here?

DOLORES. You've been stopping in the sick room, an't you Norma? She woke me up. Scared me half to death.

MARY. What's wrong, Norma?

DOLORES. She was going through me bag. I says 'Norma, what you lost'? Then she pulls me covers off, I says 'Norma, get to bed' but she's opening me drawers, I says 'Norma, what are you doing?' and she says 'he's here, I know he's here.' So we thought we'd look in your room.

NORMA. Have you got him?

MARY. Who?

NORMA. Have they put him in with you?

QUEENIE. Sit her down.

MARY *guides* NORMA *to the bed and sits her down.*

NORMA. They took him, you see. They took him so quick.

MARY. Who, Norma?

NORMA. Blue eyes.

MARY. When?

NORMA. I was in the white room. They were shouting . . .
'lie flat, lift your legs, bend your knees, pull up . . . bear
down . . . bear down . . . down . . . and there he was.
'A boy', they said. And they took him.

MARY. Didn't you hold him?

NORMA. I could hear him cry.

MARY. They must have let her hold him?

NORMA. They put him with the others. There were lots of
them crying but I knew when it was him.

MARY. You didn't even see him?

NORMA. And I know why.

MARY. Why?

NORMA. Because I can't make a nappy.

QUEENIE. She's been on the ale.

NORMA. And they wouldn't show me how. I kept asking but
they won't show me how.

MARY. You won't need to, Norma. The thing is ...

NORMA. Listen.

MARY. What?

NORMA. He's crying. Can't you hear? He's crying.

QUEENIE. Right! Doll?

   QUEENIE *finds a towel and lays it flat.*

DOLORES. What?

QUEENIE. On your back, love.

MARY. What are you doing?

DOLORES *lies down on the towel.* QUEENIE *demonstrates how to make a nappy.*

QUEENIE. Legs in the air; peg on the nose; clean the mucky bum. Slap a bit a cream on so it don't get sore.

DOLORES. You're tickling.

QUEENIE. Open legs, wider please, you know you can . . .

NORMA *starts to laugh. Unnoticed by the girls, the door opens. Enter* MATRON, *who watches the proceedings.*

QUEENIE. Fold once, twice, pin through nappy, not leg of baby. Fold once and twice and pin again. Pull baby up, dip dummy in gin, stick in gob and . . .

For the dummy, QUEENIE *uses the handle of a hairbrush.*

MATRON. On your feet.

The girls stand to attention.

MATRON. Dolores? Take Norma back to the sick room.

NORMA. Is he there?

DOLORES. Can I stay with her?

MATRON. It's past your bedtime.

DOLORES. She's upset.

MATRON. For tonight.

DOLORES. Thank you, Matron.

MATRON. And tonight only.

Exit DOLORES *and* NORMA. MATRON *picks up* QUEENIE'*s cigarettes and lighter from the floor.*

MARY. Why can't she see him?

MATRON *goes to the Dansette.*

Why can't she hold him?

MATRON *unplugs the Dansette but* MARY *stops her.*

And why don't you take your hands off what's mine?

MATRON. Get to bed.

MARY. You're not having it, do you hear me? It's mine.

MATRON. We'll discuss this in the morning.

MARY. I won't be here in the morning.

QUEENIE. Where are you going?

MARY. She can't keep me here. No-one can.

MATRON. So where will you go? Home?

MARY. No.

MATRON. Then where will you go? What will you do? How will you live?

MARY. I'll find a way.

MATRON. You're nineteen and alone, Mary. There is no other way.

MARY. Are you a mother, Matron?

MATRON. Are you?

MARY. I know how it feels.

MATRON. But have you got what it needs?

MARY *puts her hand on her heart.*

MARY. I've got everything – in here.

MATRON. But what can you give him out there?

MARY. Love.

MATRON. Believe me child, it's not enough.

MARY. And what do you know of love?

MATRON. More than you'll learn from any record.

MARY *pulls her suitcase from under her bed.*

MARY. I pity you, Matron. You'll never understand.

MATRON. If you say so.

Exit MATRON, *shutting the door.*

QUEENIE. You're acting like a kid.

MARY. I'm growing up fast.

QUEENIE. There's no buses at this time of night.

MARY. I'll walk.

QUEENIE. All the way home?

MARY. Aren't you listening? I'm not going home.

QUEENIE. You're nine months gone, where else can you go?

MARY. Eastbourne.

QUEENIE. You'll not get no further than the end of the lane.

MARY. Are you trying to stop me?

QUEENIE. I'm telling you kid, it's a dead end.

MARY. I'll get through.

   MARY *feels a sharp pain but continues packing.*

QUEENIE. And how will you get out the house? She locks
   every door at night.

MARY. I'll break a window and run. Now will you stop asking
   questions and pack up my singles?

QUEENIE. You're not taking 'em?

MARY. 'Course I am.

QUEENIE. You can't leave me here without them songs.

   MARY *stops packing and looks at* QUEENIE.

MARY. Come with me.

QUEENIE. Get off.

MARY. We'll sing them all day, every day, if we want to.

QUEENIE. So a miracle happens and we make it to the coast.
   Then what?

MARY. We'll find a seaside flat, get jobs in a hotel. Me on the
   early shift, you on lates. Whoever's not working plays
   Mum.

QUEENIE. Someone'd stop us.

MARY. They can't touch us if we're paying our way.

QUEENIE. Nah . . .

MARY. Why not?

QUEENIE. 'Cos you'd bag a bloke and I'd be out on my ear.

MARY. Who's going to take on me and a kid? Like you said, Queenie – I'm a bad girl. So I might as well act like one.

MARY shuts her case and puts on her coat.

Well?

QUEENIE. Well, it's no fun being bad on your own, is it?

QUEENIE grabs her coat and puts it on.

MARY. Is that all you're taking?

QUEENIE. I'm carrying you, aren't I?

MARY picks up the suitcase awkwardly.

MARY. *(feeling a pain)* Ow . . .

QUEENIE takes the case from MARY and heads for the door.

QUEENIE. Give it here.

MARY. You can start your career. Form a group.

QUEENIE. The Queenettes.

MARY. Queenie and the Crown Jewels.

QUEENIE. I'll crown you in a minute.

QUEENIE tries the door but it doesn't open.

MARY. It sticks.

QUEENIE. It's locked.

MARY tries the door.

QUEENIE. Holy bloody cow!

MARY. Try the window.

QUEENIE. We're in the attic.

MARY. There's an iron drainpipe.

QUEENIE. In your condition?

MARY. She can't do this.

QUEENIE. She can do what she wants.

MARY. And so can we.

QUEENIE. Who told you that?

    QUEENIE *then* MARY *takes off her coat.*

MARY. First thing in the morning, we're out.

QUEENIE. 'Course we are.

    QUEENIE *gets into bed.*

MARY. Queenie?

QUEENIE. Just play summat that'll send us to sleep.

    MARY *opens her case, takes out 'So Young' by The Ronettes and puts it on.* MARY *gets into bed and listens to the record.*

MARY. How does she do that with her voice?

QUEENIE. Mary?

MARY. How does she do that with her hair?

QUEENIE. I can't sing, can I?

MARY. What sort of question is that?

QUEENIE. The kind you ask when the lights are out.

MARY. 'Course you can.

QUEENIE. Truth – and nothing but?

    Pause.

MARY. No.

QUEENIE. Ta.

    The record plays.

MARY. Queen?

QUEENIE. I'm not bothered.

MARY. Get in.

QUEENIE *gets into* MARY*'s bed as the record plays.*

QUEENIE. I saw 'em, you know? The Ronettes. Lad I knew were mad on The Stones, they were supporting.

MARY. Queen . . .

QUEENIE. I were stood so close, I could have touched her.

MARY. Something hurts . . .

QUEENIE. You what?

MARY *breathes heavily.*

MARY. It's all right.

QUEENIE. Has it gone?

MARY. Yes.

Pause.

No. Something really hurts.

QUEENIE. What do you mean hurts?

MARY. Like cramp but worse.

QUEENIE *gets out of bed and turns the record off.*

QUEENIE. It's the excitement.

MARY. It doesn't feel like excitement.

QUEENIE *bangs on the door.*

QUEENIE. Matron?

MARY. It feels like ....

QUEENIE. Nerves and excitement and . . .

MARY. It's coming!

QUEENIE. Are you sure?

MARY. I don't know, I've never had one.

QUEENIE. If it is, you'll be all right. If it is, you've got hours.

MARY. I want to go home.

QUEENIE. We'll just keep our heads and sit tight 'til morning.

MARY *cries out in pain and* QUEENIE *bangs the door again.*

QUEENIE. Matron? Get here!

MARY. She won't hear us.

QUEENIE. Doll's underneath.

QUEENIE *stamps on the floor.*

MARY. She's gone to the sick room.

QUEENIE. There's nowt to worry about. You'll take all night.

MARY. How do you know?

QUEENIE. Shut up.

MARY. You shut up.

QUEENIE. You've gotta save your strength for what's to come.

MARY. We're fine . . . It's nature . . . Mother did it . . . Granny did it . . . we'll do it . . . you won't hurt me, will you . . . you won't hurt me cos you love me . . . you won't hurt me . . . You won't do anything to . . .

QUEENIE *starts singing the chorus of 'Chapel of Love'.*

MARY. We'll go hospital then make our way to Eastbourne . . . find a flat . . . start afresh . . . I've got ten pounds . . . ten pounds in the Post Office . . . Ten pounds should get us started . . . Oh, Mother . . .

QUEENIE. Pack it in . . .

MARY. Mother . . . !

QUEENIE. You've got hours yet.

MARY. And how the hell do you know?

QUEENIE. 'Cos I've had one, all right? I've had one.

Scene Ten

Dormitory. MARY *is holding a newborn baby under bloodstained sheets.* QUEENIE *sits on the edge of the bed.*

MARY. How old were you?

QUEENIE. Sixteen.

MARY. Did you love him?

QUEENIE. Would have done owt for him – and I did. I believed in him when he said I'd be all right.

MARY. What did you do?

QUEENIE. Told me mam. What now, I said? 'Sling yer hook'. He spoke to his. She set us up lovely in her back room. The baby slept lovely in the bottom drawer.

MARY. What's his name?

QUEENIE. William Thomas Burns. Dead bright. Crawling at five months. Into everything. Like his Dad.

MARY. You had him for five months?

QUEENIE. I had him for nine. He was walking at nine, would you believe?

MARY. That's good.

QUEENIE. Then his Dad got banged up for summat and nowt. I had to get a job so his mam took Billy on. She'd put him to bed by the time I got home. And then I wanted to go dancing. His mam said it was best for him to know me as a sister.

MARY. And where is he now?

QUEENIE. *(taps her head)* In here.

MARY. You loved him, didn't you?

QUEENIE. Couldn't help it.

MARY. Is that why you left him?

QUEENIE. I didn't leave him. I just let them take him.

MARY. It'll be different this time.

QUEENIE. It will. You can't miss what you've never had.

Sound of the door unlocking. Enter MATRON.

MATRON. Oh Lord. Is it . . .

MARY. She's asleep.

MATRON. Let me see.

QUEENIE. We cut the cord then nursed her to sleep.

MATRON. How?

QUEENIE. Nail scissors. And for once, we were glad of the chamber pot.

MATRON. And you've tied it off?

QUEENIE. I've done my best.

MATRON. Queenie – fetch towels, hot water and call an ambulance.

MATRON *reaches for the baby but* MARY *shields her.*

MARY. No.

MATRON. Mary, this is serious.

MARY. She's all right.

MATRON. There's too much at stake.

MARY. She's all right with me.

MATRON. She could bleed to death. Is that what you want?

MARY. Where she goes, I go.

MARY *curls her arms around the baby.* QUEENIE *sits down with her.*

QUEENIE. She's right, you know. The longer you hold her, the harder it'll be.

MARY. Harder to what?

QUEENIE. To let her go.

Pause.

MARY. I thought you were on my side?

QUEENIE. I am.

MARY. We're running away?

QUEENIE. Face it, love. We're going nowhere.

MARY. We can now she's born.

QUEENIE. Don't you think if there was any other way, I'd have found it. I'd have Billy with me now. Every day, I tell myself I'll go and get him back.

MARY. There's no-one to stop you.

QUEENIE. And there's nowhere to go.

MARY. There has to be somewhere.

QUEENIE. If there was, do you think I'd be here?

MARY. You mean I've never had a choice?

QUEENIE. Come on, now . . .

QUEENIE *holds her hands out for the baby.*

MARY. Will I know her, do you think? If I see her in the street?

QUEENIE. It's time.

MARY. Her name's Lucy.

MARY *hands the baby to* QUEENIE, *who hands her to* MATRON. *Exit* MARY, *in tears.*

QUEENIE. I'm right, aren't I? There in't nowhere?

MATRON. I wish there was.

QUEENIE. I'll run her a bath.

MATRON. I'll call the doctor.

QUEENIE. What will you tell him?

MATRON. That's not your concern.

QUEENIE *turns to go.*

You did well.

QUEENIE. Did I?

MATRON. I was called to a house in the middle of the night. A long time ago. A fourteen year old girl had given birth in her bedroom. Bitten the cord. Couldn't stop it bleeding. A few minutes more, it might have been different. I was only your age.

QUEENIE. Maybe I've been good for summat, after all?

MATRON. See to your friend.

Exit QUEENIE, *followed by* MATRON.

Scene Eleven

Study. Ten days later. MRS ADAMS *sits waiting. Enter* MATRON.

MATRON. I'm so sorry to have kept you waiting.

MRS ADAMS. Is it Mary?

MATRON. A young lady turned up on the doorstep with a suitcase. It's fortuitous for her that Mary leaves today.

MRS ADAMS. Where is she?

MATRON. In her room.

MRS ADAMS. And she's . . .

MATRON. On the mend. Have you come from the hospital?

MRS ADAMS. I stopped by. She's gaining weight, they say.

MATRON. The doctor was here within the hour. He found her none the worse for her ordeal.

MRS ADAMS. You'd wouldn't even know to look at her.

MATRON. She's a bonny girl.

MRS ADAMS. Strong little fingers, too.

MATRON. She's got spirit, that's for sure.

MATRON *hands* MRS ADAMS *an envelope.*

MRS ADAMS *(reading)*. Room 205.

MATRON. Second floor. Straight down the corridor, then left.

MRS ADAMS. When we go, will we see them?

MATRON. They'll be waiting elsewhere. You won't have to take her through.

MRS ADAMS. But I'd rather.

MATRON. It's not advisable.

MRS ADAMS. I only want to express my gratitude.

MATRON. Believe me, they know.

MRS ADAMS. Have you met them, Matron?

MATRON. They paid us a visit.

MRS ADAMS. Are they nice?

MATRON. They're a childless couple from Devon. Late thirties. Ten years married. She can't carry full-term.

MRS ADAMS. We had some lovely holidays in Devon. When Mary was . . .

MRS ADAMS *'s voice breaks.*

MATRON. Would you like a glass of water?

MRS ADAMS. No, thank you.

MATRON. You can take your daughter home today. Put it all behind you.

MRS ADAMS. The house has been so quiet without her.

MATRON. I'm sure.

MRS ADAMS. We had a long wait for Mary, Mr Adams and I. At least we know she won't have that trouble.

MARY. You'll be grandparents one day, I've no doubt about that.

MRS ADAMS. 1931, we were married. Set up home in a rented room and just assumed it'd happen. We were both from big families but we'd set our hearts on two. A boy for my husband, a girl for me. A couple of years passed but we weren't unduly worried. With both of us working, we could save for a house. After seven years married, I went to the doctor. Keep trying, he said. Then the war came along. My husband went to Burma, he won't speak of it still. But he came home on leave, for a night before he left and I really don't know why I'm telling you this.

MATRON. I lost my husband at Dunkirk.

MRS ADAMS. You were married?

MATRON. Just a year. Please go on .

MRS ADAMS. I've lost my thread.

MATRON. He came home.

MRS ADAMS. For a night before he left. I mistook the first signs for missing him. But nine months later came a miracle. Mary Elizabeth, named after our mothers'. I didn't know such happiness was possible. We've not had it easy, what with one thing and another. We've not had it easy but for Mary.

MATRON. You do know, Mrs Adams, that once adoption takes place it's irreversible?

MRS ADAMS. Of course.

MATRON. Forgive me Mrs Adams but I'm duty-bound to ask; are you absolutely sure it's what you want?

MRS ADAMS *considers her reply.*

MRS ADAMS. They don't look kindly on these girls where we come from. Not kindly at all, I'm afraid. I've seen how they're treated, I know what they're called and while there's breath in my body, they won't do that to Mary. Not to my little girl – and to not hers. It has to be.

MATRON *stands and gestures for* MRS ADAMS *to leave.*

MATRON. After you.

Exit MRS ADAMS *and* MATRON.

Scene Twelve

Dormitory. MARY *packs her suitcase, which lies open on the bed.* DOLORES *passes items to her as she packs.*

DOLORES. 'Ey, Mary? That new lass nearly passed out when she saw your sheets. We had 'er on you'd done someone in.

MARY *continues packing.*

Do you think Norma's feeling better?

MARY. I'm sure she is.

DOLORES. Will you go and see her?

MARY. I don't know where she lives.

DOLORES. You'd best write me your address. So I can ask you to the wedding.

MARY *takes a pen and paper out of her suitcase and gives it to* DOLORES.

MARY. Why don't you give me yours?

DOLORES. Will you send us a letter?

MARY. If you like.

DOLORES. *(beaming)* I never get a letter.

DOLORES *sits down to write her address.* MARY *closes the suitcase. Enter* QUEENIE, *who watches* MARY *from the doorway.*

MARY. All right?

QUEENIE. You've forgot your gloves.

MARY. They're in the case.

QUEENIE. She'll want you in your gloves.

MARY. I'd like to introduce you.

QUEENIE. No, ta.

MARY. To break the ice. For when you come to stay.

QUEENIE. Doll? We're wanted in the kitchen.

DOLORES *hands* MARY *the pen and paper.*

DOLORES. I don't mind you going now you're doing me a letter.

MARY. Good.

DOLORES. Can I do you one back?

MARY. If you like.

DOLORES. I'll start it tonight.

Exit DOLORES, *followed by* QUEENIE.

MARY. Queenie?

QUEENIE. I've got work to do.

MARY *writes down her address and offers it to* QUEENIE.

MARY. My address.

QUEENIE *looks at it then hands it back.*

QUEENIE. Mapperley Park. Sounds posh.

MARY. You will come?

QUEENIE. That'd get the nets twitching.

MARY. I need you to come.

QUEENIE. Won't I give the game away?

MARY. You're the only one I can talk to.

QUEENIE. It's best forgot. All of it.

MARY. How?

QUEENIE. You'll find a way.

MARY. I don't blame you for saying what you said. Not after Billy.

QUEENIE. Who's Billy?

MARY. Your son.

MARY *offers her address again.* QUEENIE *refuses it.*

Enter MATRON *and* MRS ADAMS. *Exit* QUEENIE.

MRS ADAMS. Mary?

MARY. Mother.

MATRON. Nearly done?

MARY. Not quite, Matron.

MRS ADAMS. Nearly done.

MARY. How was your journey?

MRS ADAMS. Rather slow.

MARY. Is Father . . .

MRS ADAMS. Glad to hear your Aunt's on the mend.

MRS ADAMS *gets* MARY *'s coat and holds it open for her.*

MRS ADAMS. I've spoken to the bank. You start a new job on Monday.

MARY. This Monday?

MRS ADAMS. City centre branch, no less.

MARY. I liked it where I was.

MRS ADAMS. We've been rather busy since you've been away. Father took the opportunity to decorate your room.

MARY. It was a girl, Mother.

MARY *puts on her coat.*

MRS ADAMS. Button up, Mary.

MARY. I held her.

MRS ADAMS. You don't want to feel the cold.

MARY. I kept her warm 'til morning.

MRS ADAMS. Come along, Mary. You're a big girl, now.

MARY *puts the Dansette and records on* QUEENIE*'s bed.*

MARY. For Queenie.

MATRON. I'd rather you took it.

MARY. So she doesn't forget.

MRS ADAMS. The taxi's waiting.

MARY. I'm not ready.

MRS ADAMS. Then let me help you.

MARY. No, Mother. I'll follow you down.

MATRON. Shall I show you out?

MARY. She knows the way.

MRS ADAMS. Mary?

MATRON. It's all right. I'll bring her down.

Exit MRS ADAMS.

MATRON. Well?

MARY. Not really.

MATRON. You will be.

MARY. If you say so.

MATRON. It's over, Mary. Time to go home.

MARY *hands her teddy bear to* MATRON.

MARY. For Lucy. My baby.

MATRON *takes the teddy bear. Exit* MARY. MATRON
holds the teddy bear as 'Be My Baby' plays to blackout.

The End.